Easy
Mandalas

by

Tabz Jones

©TabzJones

©TabzJones

©TabzJones

©TabzJones

©TabzJones

©TabzJones

©TabzJones

©TabzJones

©TabzJones

©TabzJones

©TabzJones

Thank you

for your purchase!

To see the full catalog of my art, don't forget
to stop by
www.gothictoggs.net